After School Activities Your Kids Will Enjoy

TABLE OF CONTENTS

INTRODUCTION

It has often been said that if children came with their own set of instructions, parenting would be a whole lot easier. While this might be true, it wouldn't be as challenging, and it sure wouldn't be nearly as much fun!

Since there aren't definitive instruction booklets for parenting and no two children are alike, parents have to wing it as they go along. This can create some incredible memories and make the job the toughest one a person will ever love.

Engaging children in activities they love can be one of the most frustrating challenges facing parents today. Ask many parents and they will readily admit they have no idea what to do with their children once school is out, the homework is done and the chores have all been completed. The problem becomes even more troublesome during vacations and especially during that long stretch of summer.

Of course, there are alternatives the kids love, but parents aren't so fond of. The truth is educational, recreational and low-tech activities do experience constant competition from electronics like video games and television sets.

While the "electronic babysitters" can work as a reward or an occasional activity, most parents just don't want their kids sitting in front of a screen all the time. These activities are just not healthy for children on a constant basis. They do need to get up, stretch their legs and expand their mind.

For some parents, the problem after school doesn't involve computers or television programs. Their kids would rather "hang out" with their friends and remain unsupervised for hours on end. This is an issue that can also cause parents a great deal of angst.

Just like television and video games, hanging out (with supervision) can be great once in a while. It is important for building socialization skills and helping kids unwind after busy days at school. Still, when this is the only after-school activity offered, it can be a big problem.

There has to be better options for parents to try that kids will like, right? Well, there is. In fact, you'll find with a little bit of exploration and some nudging, you can locate the perfect after-school activities to keep your kids engaged, enjoying themselves and staying out of trouble at the same time.

If you're ready to take the after-school activity bull by the horns and find things for your kids to do that will actually engage them, read on. In this book, we'll discuss the importance of having activities lined up, how to explore choices for younger children and even teens and even offer some ideas for the entire family.

It is important to remember that after-school activities don't have to be all solo ventures. If parents and other children can get involved, too, the time spent can become doubly valuable. Not only will youngsters be engaged in a healthy activity, they'll also benefit from family time and bonding.

There's more to life once the bell rings than sitting on a couch or watching a computer screen. Help your kids find activities that suit them and you will be doing your children and yourself a huge favor.

As you search out activities to keep your kids busy after school, do keep them in the loop. Ideally, you'll want to find something to do that truly interests them. Whether it's a project or hobby they can tackle at home or a more organized undertaking, their input can be vital for your success. When you find something you can both agree upon, your child will benefit and so will your peace of mind.

Remember though that no two kids are alike, so the process of finding something that can click might take some effort. What works for the boy down the street or your co-worker's daughter might not suit your child to a T. This particular challenge, once met, will pay off for you with a happier child and less worry on your part.

With any luck, the activities you find will even make the long stretches of summer look less intimidating!

WHY AFTER-SCHOOL ACTIVITIES MATTER SO MUCH

Just about every parent has seen the horror story headlines about kids who are left alone to their own devices after school. When supervision isn't high and kids aren't engaged after school, all kinds of bad things can happen. Even good kids can slip up and get into big trouble.

There are also issues that can arise with children who are supervised, but not necessarily engaged. Mom or Dad can be at home with the kids every day after school, but the youngsters can still be bored. This can lead to behavioral problems and an atmosphere that is just not pleasant for anyone to be in. Once homework and chores are done, many kids just need more than television or video games to entertain and engage them.

A study performed by the New York Chapter of Fight Crime: Invest in Kids showed that children who are left unsupervised for several days a week are seven times more likely than their supervised counterparts to become the victims of crime. The same study concluded that kids who are engaged in after-school activities are also less likely to commit crimes themselves, do drugs and engage in sexual behavior.

Beyond the horror stories, which aren't representative of every kid that's left alone to play video games or watch TV after school, there are other very compelling reasons why keeping them busy makes sense.

A number of studies have been done that show the benefits of after-school activities. Some of the prospective benefits youngsters and teens enjoy when they take part in programs or even pursue hobbies at home include:

- **Boosted self-esteem**
  Organized sports, working on hobbies at home, dance, educational clubs and other activities can all give children a sense of belonging and esteem. The accomplishments that go along with many activities can be incredible boosters on this front. The self-esteem youngsters learn to feel in after-school activities can, and often does, translate into other areas of life. At the very least, it can give them the willingness to try new things.

- **Better socialization skills**
  When children take part in organized activities with other

youngsters, they learn to build their socialization skills. They can also benefit from the team-building skills that are learned in sports and other similar activities. In addition, they can end up making lifelong friends that share similar, positive interests.

- **Better academic performance**
  Children who are engaged in activities they love tend to perform better in school. This can be due to a number of reasons, including the confidence builder that an activity can provide and also the desire to be allowed to continue in the extracurricular activity. Beloved after-school activities can be powerful motivators for improved academic performance. They can also help youngsters build their academic skills outside of the classroom and teach them lessons that will last a lifetime.

- **Lowered risks**
  As supported by the New York study, it has been found that children who are kept busy after school are less likely to engage in criminal and other harmful activities. They are also much less likely to be victimized themselves. In addition, children who enjoy their after-school activities are less likely to suffer from depression or have behavioral problems in school or out of it.

- **Improved physicality**
  While not all after-school activities are physical in nature, many are. Organized sports and other physical pursuits can help children get in shape and stay that way. The lessons learned can put a youngster on the right path early in life when it comes to caring for health and exercising. It's a simple fact that childhood obesity is a big problem. After-school activities of certain types can help combat this issue.

- **Resume building**
  While activities for very young children might not apply for future resumes, many teen activities do. Boy Scouts who receive higher rankings, teens who volunteer and even athletes that really excel can build their college credentials and even career resumes while they stay engaged after school.

- **Increased responsibility**
  When children take part in after-school activities, they have to learn to juggle school work with "play time." This can be an incredible force for teaching them responsibility and self-discipline.

While it's not necessary to book every second of every day outside of school with an organized or productive activity, making sure children have something to do that's positive can have very big impacts on their lives. Even young children can benefit from engaging activities that take place outside the traditional classroom. Teens and preteens, in particular, tend to shine when the right fit is found.

Selecting the right activity for the child in question, however, can be very important. Don't fool yourself on this point. If a child is forced into a hobby that he or she doesn't like or finds too difficult to pursue, some of the benefits will go away. While supervision might be provided, the chance for growth and expression will not be. With this in mind, it is imperative to select activities with care.

SELECTING THE RIGHT ACTIVITIES

Suzy takes ballet. Tommy goes to karate. Jimmy has to be dropped off at soccer practice. Caroline has Girl Scouts.

If you've hung around parents with busy kids, you know the scheduling can be downright insane. Trying to make sure everyone gets to where they need to go after school can be an exercise worthy of a logistics expert. Still, many parents make it work one way or another.

Why? Is it really worth going to that much trouble when putting all the kids in the same activity would make life so much easier for the parents?

While having to be in four different places on the same night might not be the wisest choice, giving kids the ability to choose – to an extent – their own path when it comes to after-school activities is important.

Remember, no two kids are alike. Suzy might excel at ballet, but Caroline could have two left feet. Tommy might love the discipline of karate and Jimmy the team spirit of soccer. Letting them explore the things that appeal to them and that they are actually good at can help you and them reap all the benefits of after-school activities.

Do keep in mind that not every good, rewarding after-school activity has to be organized, costly or even require classes. Your children might love to create works of art or simply want to build model cars with dad. It could be they want to spend time learning how to cook or taking up gardening. Let them assist you in selecting activities, and the options that come up might just surprise you.

Still, you will want to guide the process. There are keys to helping them and you find the perfect activities after school that can engage them and help them grow. Some of the basic rules of the road to keep in mind as you consider the options available at home and in your community include these below.

THE AGE OF THE CHILDREN

In order to gain the benefits that activities can provide, the selection should be age appropriate, or at least universal. Putting very young children into organized after-school activities every day of the week, for example, might be too much. While they might have fun a day a week or even two, keep in mind they've been away from you at school. They might want some kid and mom or dad time, too. Also, do keep in mind the ability level of the child in question. A kindergartener might adore the idea of taking beginning painting, but lessons that are technically geared for older children might actually serve to discourage them rather than encourage them. Teens, too, will not generally benefit from activities that are geared too low for their level. There are, however, plenty of activities that can be described as "universal." This means they can be altered to suit any age. We'll talk about some ideas on this front a little later.

THE SKILLS AND/OR INTERESTS OF THE CHILD

It is important to try and match up children with after-school activities. Forcing a child who is terrified of large animals to take horseback riding lessons, for example, can be a very bad idea. Pay attention to the natural skills of the youngster in question, the things they tend to gravitate toward and even the activities their friends are engaged in. Nudging in one direction or another is okay. Forcing a teenage boy who loves basketball, but hates football, to toss the pigskin five nights a week because Dad did will likely only backfire on you.

THE COSTS INVOLVED

While most parents would love to say yes to just about any after-school activity that keeps kids out of trouble and having fun, sometimes the options just aren't feasible. Do pay attention to the costs involved and carefully size up the pricing before giving a green light. Hockey, for example, might seem like a cheap sport to take up, but this is not necessarily the case. Do your homework as a parent before you move forward. If your child is really hooked on a particular activity and you cannot afford it, consider other alternatives. Some sports leagues offer scholarships. Community-based programs in art might be cheaper than sending your daughter to night classes for teens at a college campus. There are often ways around the financial obstacles, but you will have to seek them out.

YOUR CHILD'S DESIRES

While it's okay for you to choose to put your 3-year-old in ballet classes, making your teen learn how to play the piano when his heart is set on the guitar might not serve you or your child well. Do ask your child what activities are of interest and see if there is a way to accommodate. If your child is a "serial hobbyist" and likes to jump from activity to activity, check into trial classes or at-home opportunities for learning or trying something out first. Ideally, though, you will want to find an activity that fits the child in question. If you do so, it will be more likely that your child's interest will be held and the benefits activities can deliver will be realized.

YOUR SCHEDULE

Signing your son up for soccer and then never being able to get him there won't do anyone any good. If you are both leaning toward outside, organized activities or lessons, do make sure the activity and program selected fit into your schedule, too.

Picking after-school activities for kids is not necessarily an easy task. Take some time on this front and put a little thought into it. Your children don't necessarily have to be in elaborate programs to reap the rewards either.

KEEPING YOUNGER CHILDREN BUSY

Finding after-school activities for younger children can be a little less of a challenge than picking out programs or pursuits for teenagers. Still, it is important to exercise as much care on this front. Little ones will often require a careful balance of school time, fun time and down time. Push them too hard and their school work or your home life can suffer.

The fact of the matter is that little ones can benefit from after-school activities. Organized programs, for example, can help them build important skills as they work on socialization even more. At-home activities can keep them off the computer or away from the television set. In either case, you win and so do they.

When you select out-of-home programs for younger children, the points we discussed before can all come into play. There are a few other things you might want to keep in mind when making the choices, too. They include:

- **The level of commitment involved**
  Parents are often floored by the amount of pressure and commitment that some after-school activities for very young children call for. Cheerleading programs, team sports and other similar activities that might have a competitive side could call for more commitment than you or your little one might be willing to give. While learning about responsibility is great at any age, your 5-year-old might not appreciate having to report for practice three nights a week before a big dance competition. If you're not willing to stick with it or are very concerned that she won't be, consider something else.

- **The time involved**
  Going for a 7 p.m. ball practice might sound like no real problem to you, but if your 6-year-old is used to going to bed at 8, his school work could suffer. Keep the times that programs start in mind when signing kids up for anything. While turning in after bedtime is okay once in a while, a regular diet of it could actually hurt your child more than the program helps.

Younger children can benefit from after-school activities as much as their older counterparts. Keep in mind, however, that important activities do not always have to take place outside the home. Weigh the options, your child's interests and even the costs and time involved before setting something in stone. You will find there are plenty of options for young children both in organized activities and things that can be done at home.

Don't be surprised if very little children would rather spend time at home doing something fun with you after school. If this is the case, enjoy it while you can!

EDUCATIONAL ACTIVITIES THAT ARE ACTUALLY FUN

Younger children don't always require organized activities to gain some real rewards. If you'd rather engage them at home and use after-school time for fun while you sneak in little lessons, there are plenty of things you can pursue together. If you have the time and the inclination, there are some educational activities that can keep your little one busy, having fun and learning a ton in the process without even realizing it.

Some of the things you can do at home to mix things up, have fun and teach them some important lessons along the way include:

- **Cooking together**
  No, you don't want to turn a kindergartener loose in your kitchen! You can, however, ask him to help you bake cookies, prepare dinner or even make a cake. As you work on a recipe, break out things that he can actually do without too much trouble. Work on counting the number of cups of water that go into a batter or how many steaks are needed to feed the family. This is a great way to work on basic math while giving your little one some fun time with you.

- **Science time**
  Get a microscope, magnifying glass or camera and go on an exploration of the "scientific world." Let your child look at a drop of tap water under the microscope. Ask her to take pictures of the "wildlife" in your backyard. Use a magnifying glass to see harmless bugs and creepy crawlies up close and personal. You can even use your computer to try and identify the things you've seen together.

- **Worksheets**
  The Internet is loaded with Web sites provided by early childhood educators. Do a search for fun worksheets they can color or fill out to help with the skills they are building in school. Try to keep this

time fun time though by pulling out "gold star" stickers and other rewards.

- **Scavenger hunts**
  Have your child go on a "scavenger hunt" in the house looking for objects that start with a certain letter. This is a great way to help them connect the alphabet they are learning in school with the words they use every day. It can also be a whole lot of fun and it might just surprise you how much they know!

You don't necessarily have to be elaborate with after-school activities to have an impact on a young child. Even small projects can keep them busy, engaged, learning and having fun. Sometimes, however, you might find that organized activities fit them or your schedule better.

GETTING CREATIVE AT HOME

After-school activities don't have to be blatantly educational, terribly structured or even organized to have a big impact on younger children. Sometimes a little creativity can go a long way. If your child or children love getting into art projects, this preference can provide the perfect springboard for keeping them busy and engaged after school.

Keep in mind that artistic expression can, in fact, lead to great things academically down the road. Children who pursue the arts tend to do better in school. According to Americans for the Arts, the benefits of artistic pursuits can be many. They include:

- Stimulating critical thinking;

- Improving developmental growth;

- Encouraging a sense of craftsmanship;

- Encouraging the development of goal-setting skills;

- Teaching self-expression;

- Boosting self-confidence.

There are a number of things you can do at home to help children express their creativity. From small-scale projects just to pass the time to large-scale ventures, there are plenty of opportunities. Depending on the direction your child's artistic leanings take, you can even turn your at-home fun into an organized activity down the road.

Some of the things you can do together with a creative flair to them include:

- **Basic arts and crafts**
  Let them draw, paint, work with clay or safe play dough after school. Give them ideas on what to do or just let them go crazy inside their own imaginations. Try to keep projects that are planned challenging, but fun and do mix up the mediums used to keep them engaged.

- **Larger crafts projects**
  It's also possible to set them to work doing slightly larger crafts projects. Have them create centerpieces for holidays, special dinners or anytime occasions. Get them busy making poster board murals for their rooms or to give as gifts. The Internet is great source of ideas for larger scale projects that can let their sense of creativity flow.

- **Musical ventures**
  If your child loves music, use this to keep them busy after school. Have music time where he gets to play instruments. These can be as basic as pots and pans or as elaborate as a full sized piano. Let him have fun and create. If he's a little more advanced, consider getting video courses you can take together to explore an instrument more fully before diving into actual classes. You can also use music time to explore different style of music. Play your favorites and explore his. Tune the radio into something neither of you normally listen to and see what you like or don't like about different styles.

- **Gotta dance**
  If your child adores dancing, let her have some fun with it. Turn on some music and have a blast making up moves. Get some videos and see if you can copy the steps. Dance time is great for expressing creativity and it can also serve as a wonderful source of exercise for both of you.

Creative expression is a great way to pass the time after school. When you let them enjoy the arts at their own pace, you can help them develop a lifelong appreciation for music, fine arts and dance. There are, however, other forms of expressionism that can work very well for engaging young children after school.

THE POWER OF IMAGINATION

One of the biggest things that separates children from adults is little ones' ability to tap into their imaginations to pass the time. Use this to your advantage and theirs when it's time to have some fun once classes are over. Encouraging them to use their imaginations can help them develop skills that may last a lifetime.

Some of the activities you can use to help encourage them in more imaginative pursuits include:

- **Storytelling**
  Create verbal stories together with your child or children. Start out a story with a few lines and then let them pick up. You can do this in round-robin style or let your child take over and see where the story goes from there. Encourage the use of "out of the box" ideas and descriptions.

- **Puppet shows**
  If your child loves creating on a number of different fronts, you can enjoy projects that span multiple days and many arts. Create puppets as an "art project" one day or over the course of several. Once this is done, work on some stories related to the puppets. Let your child create the entire script if he or she is so inclined. If not, pitch in and lend a hand. Once these things are done, you can put on a show for the entire family. If you're really inspired, create a stage and set that relates to the theme using a big cardboard box and some crayons and markers.

- **Role playing and other similar pursuits**
  Children not only love to use their imaginations, but they also love to cast themselves into different roles. Encourage them to play house, detective, teacher or whatever their hearts' desire. Cast yourself in a role, too, and show them that "big people" think imagination is important, too. Let them set the rules, within reason, and remember to have some fun together.

A child's imagination is a playground just waiting to be explored. Let them express it and you will enjoy some experiences together that are amazing, rewarding and important.

HOW TO GET SOMETHING BENEFICIAL OUT OF TELEVISION TIME TOGETHER

Hands-on, educational and creative activities are excellent for younger children in the hours after school. They can be fun, rewarding and teach them skills that will translate into other areas of life. Sometimes, however, kids just want to kick back, relax and watch a little television.

Relax! This is perfectly acceptable. Television and even video games can provide a great way for your child to relax, enjoy some entertainment and even learn. If you want to help them get more out of television time or even video game time, there are things you can do as a parent.

To make the most out of the experience and increase the "value" for younger children, consider following these tips:

- **Carefully select what is acceptable**
  Remember, you are the parent and can pick what your children watch or play and what they don't watch or play. Take care when picking television shows and video games to make sure they are age-appropriate and fit your personal moral compass. There are some great shows out there for younger children that combine educational topics with pure entertainment. The same can be said for video games.

- **View materials in advance**
  If you have any reservations about a particular show or game, take the time to check it out first. This can be the best way to be 100 percent certain you agree something is appropriate for your child. It can also give you an opportunity to chew on the materials to see how they can be best turned into "quality viewing time."

- **Watch and play with your child**
  When possible, sit down and watch television shows with your child and play their games with them, too. This can actually serve as really good bonding time. On video games, try to make sure what they are playing is right for their level. Do pay close attention to these. Not all games that seem innocent turn out to be so. Some games that look "easy" to you, can also be very frustrating for younger children.

- **Consider using a mix of educational and pure entertainment vehicles**

  Remember, kids do need a break, too. Let them enjoy a cartoon for the sake of doing so once in a while. You can still help them get more out of the experience by following the next tip. When viewing educational programs, by the way, make sure they are appropriate for the age. A documentary on shark attacks might enthrall your 15-year-old, but your 5-year-old could end up with nightmares!

- **Ask them questions**

  Once you've viewed a show or played a game, turn the experience into a learning adventure. Ask them questions about what they've seen or what they've done. Make it a fun game. Let them ask you questions, too, so they can see how well you paid attention.

Television and video games are not all bad. If you want to let your children enjoy these forms of entertainment after school, it doesn't make you a bad parent. If you take a little time to make sure the materials are appropriate and even help them get more out of the experience, the "electronic babysitters" can actually prove to be incredible educational materials. At the very least, you and your child will be able to relax and enjoy some downtime together. There's nothing wrong with that!

INTRODUCING THE SPIRIT OF VOLUNTEERISM

If you like the idea of getting out of the house after school and teaching your children to give back and appreciate what they have, you'll find it's never too early for them to learn about volunteerism. There are all sorts of things you can do in your community and even in your own neighborhood.

With pre- and elementary school aged children, these ideas can help you teach them to give back while making sure they are engaged and actually get into the activity:

- **Trash patrol**

  You and your child or children can appoint yourselves the neighborhood trash patrol. Grab some garbage bags and scour your streets for trash people have tossed out of their windows. This can give your kids a sense of accomplishment, help them learn about the environment and make your neighborhood look better all at

once. This can even become an ongoing endeavor. Just make sure
you all wear gloves, stick to the side of the road and observe other
rules of safety.

- **Neighborly service**
  If you have a sick neighbor or an older neighbor who needs a little
  help, pitch in with your child's help. Assist them with household
  chores, grocery runs or even work together to make them dinner or
  a get well card.

- **Food banks**
  Local food banks and homeless shelters often need help sorting
  donations. In some cases, the jobs available are perfectly
  appropriate for little hands.

- **School projects**
  Have your children help out at PTA meetings or other events. They
  can take tickets at spaghetti dinners, hand out fliers and so on.

- **Nursing home visits**
  You and your children can become regular visitors at local nursing
  homes. Most facilities are more than happy to have youngsters
  come by and help entertain their residents. The residents
  themselves are generally delighted to get to spend time with an
  "adopted" grandchild, too. If you don't love the idea of making this
  a regular stop, shoot for holidays or other special events.

- **Seasonal drives and other programs**
  Teach your children about those who are less fortunate by
  encouraging them to give of themselves. Let them sort through
  their toys before birthdays or other holidays and pick out those that
  can be easily recycled for use by other children. They can even do
  this with their own clothing. Also consider shopping together for
  new donations that you might be interested in giving to
  organizations like Toys for Tots. This is a great way to expose your
  youngsters to the fact that not everyone has as much as they do.

- **Special events**
  Some larger charities hold special events that are perfectly
  appropriate for introducing children to volunteerism. The American
  Cancer Society's Relay For Life, for example, is an event a small
  child can take part in. While special events won't keep your child
  busy after school every day, they can serve as a springboard into
  other activities.

- **Donation drives**
  A lot of organizations cannot accept actual physical time given by

young volunteers, but your kids can still help them out. Consider having them donate money they earn through garage sales, lemonade stands and other similar ventures to a charity of their choice. For example, they might want to give to a local animal shelter or a special medical organization. Do make a big idea out of the prospect of holding a sale to make money for the charity so there's no question that the money earned will be given away and not used to purchase new toys or so on.

Teaching children to give back is a venture that can never begin too early. You can use volunteerism as a great way to pass the time after school and keep your kids engaged and learning. In many cases, you can even have a whole lot of fun in the process.

ORGANIZED ACTIVITIES CAN BE THE CHARM

While it's great to spend quality time together after school engaging in activities that are fun, educational and rewarding, sometimes this just doesn't work. Either the kids are really insistent on wanting to take part in organized activities or work schedules just don't mesh for afternoons to be filled with at-home fun. Whatever the case, organized activities can provide an incredible way to make sure they're busy and gaining something out of the experience.

Just about any organized activity out there for younger children can prove beneficial not only for helping them express their interests, but also in teaching them valuable life lessons.

Some of the more popular options for after-school fun in an organized manner include:

- **Sporting activities**
  T-ball, softball, basketball, football and other similar sports can help youngsters get active and stay that way. They can also help them learn about playing by the rules and teach them to work as part of a team. In addition, sports can be an incredible self-esteem booster and also help with socialization skills. Just make sure the child really is keen on the sport in question before diving in headlong.

- **Scouting**
  Brownies, Cub Scouts and other similar activities can be incredibly beneficial for young children. Organizations like this can expose

youngsters to a number of different areas of interest while teaching them the importance of responsibility, team work and preparation. Scouting won't necessarily take up every night of the week, but it can become a big part of a youngster's life that will carry forward for years to come.

- **Classes**
  Art, music, karate and dance classes can also serve youngsters very well. These types of pursuits will help them learn goal-setting, self-discipline and the importance of practice and patience. In some cases, recitals can even assist them in learning how to deal with public speaking or performance situations.

- **Clubs**
  After-school clubs, religious clubs and other organized group type programs can provide the perfect after-school solution for some youngsters. These organizations can help children explore their interests while giving them a chance to socialize and have fun.

Keeping youngsters busy after school doesn't have to be as hard as it sounds. There are plenty of opportunities out there to help them explore who they are, what they might like to do and the world around them. In most cases, the activities involves are a whole lot of fun – so much so they might not notice they are learning valuable life lessons as they take part.

Just remember when picking activities to keep the child's interests, age levels and abilities in mind. It's great to help them explore new things, but pigeonholing them into a pursuit they don't necessarily enjoy might backfire on you.

All in all, younger, school-age children are fairly easy to keep engaged after school. Preteens and teens, however, can present a whole different set of challenges. Get them started in activities they like when they're younger, however, and the problems might solve themselves before they even get started!

ENGAGING OLDER CHILDREN

While it can be a sanity saver to keep younger children engaged in activities after school, the prospect can be doubly important for older children. Preteens and teens, even the best of the best, can land themselves in a world of trouble if they are left to their own devices for too long. Plus, it's a simple fact that after-school activities for older kids can help them develop skills they will soon need in college and the working world that will follow.

As it is for younger children, the things that can engage older kids and keep them out of trouble can run a rather wide gamut. From pursuing hobbies at home under parental supervision to taking part in organized activities, the options are as diverse as kids themselves.

When activities are a part of everyday life for preteens and teens, the benefits can astound. Older children who are kept busy are:

- **Less likely to get into trouble**
  As we've already discussed, children who are engaged after school are not as likely to commit crimes, do drugs, drink or even engage in premarital sexual activities. When kids are kept busy, they just don't have time to get into things they shouldn't.

- **More likely to enjoy self-confidence**
  After-school activities, even hobbies pursued at home, can give older children a sense of pride and accomplishment. This can be important for helping them learn to try new things and give them the confidence to succeed in life.

- **Less likely to be victimized**
  When older kids just "hang out," they are more available to opportunities for victimization. Studies have shown that children who are engaged after school are just not as likely to become the victims of crime. This can be very comforting for you indeed!

- **More likely to learn skills that can help them**
  Organized after-school activities, volunteering and other similar pursuits can look fantastic on college and even employment applications. The skills that are learned in the after-school hours can take them just as far and sometimes farther than their SAT results. From actual career skills to better socialization and team

working skills, these things can and do translate well into lessons that can last a lifetime.

Older children can benefit from after-school activities as much and sometimes even more than their younger counterparts. The trick here is finding things they want to do, will enjoy and will actually stick with. Preteens and teens can be a real challenge on this front, but there is something out there that will do the trick. If you both work at it, you will find something they are interested in enough to keep them engaged.

The options for older kids do include many of the choices for younger children. The difference is that the activities scale up to the right level. From at-home projects you can do together to artistic and organized pursuits, the options are just diverse enough that something can be hit on that will work for your preteen or teen.

FUN, EDUCATIONAL PROJECTS

While there are all sorts of organized, after-school activities for older children that we'll discuss later, not every child is hip to get involved in these pursuits. If you are available to provide supervision in the after-school hours, there are plenty of things you can do together or even have your child do on his or her own that can fill the hours with rewarding fun that doesn't just involve sitting around and watching television.

Some of the possibilities that might be of interest to your child include:

- **Creating a collection**
  Older children are often very keen on building their own collections. Whether it's stamps, coins, musical CDs or even action figures or movies, keeping and building a collection can teach kids a lot of valuable lessons. They can learn such things as how to research purchases and value, how to create displays and how to take care of their prized possessions.

- **Photography**
  This is a hobby that a lot of kids can really sink their teeth into. Whether you arm them with a camera or video equipment, photography can help them learn to explore and observe the world around them. It can also help them explore potential career skills and even assist them in expressing themselves.

- **Local history**
  If you are available after school and your teen's a history or war buff, go on explorations locally. Chances are you have historic sites, museums and other places of interest that you can research up on together and then explore.

There are all sorts of things you and your older child can do in the after-school hours to keep them busy and having fun. In many cases, you might even be able to involve your children's friends in the pursuits.

HANDS-ON HELP

If your child's more artistically inclined or prefers to get hands-on with projects, there are all sorts of things you can consider to help them stay busy in the after-school hours. Depending on your child's personal preferences, you can help support and encourage their hands-on nature by:

- **Keeping them loaded up on arts supplies**
  A lot of preteens and teens are rather artistically inclined. If you can't get them to organized classes or they just aren't interested in learning more than they do in school, you can still encourage the pursuit by purchasing them the supplies they need. You can even further encourage artistic pursuits by helping them enter contests and even taking them places that might inspire them with new ideas.

- **Giving them projects to work on**
  Preteens and teens who are mechanically inclined will occupy themselves for weeks and months on end if they are given the right project to tackle. Give a boy a junk car to work on or a backyard tree house to build and their hours will be filled with jobs that will keep them busy and at home. In many cases, they can also involve their friends, which is great for helping you get to know them better, too.

- **Getting them into the music**
  Older children tend to go gaga over musical pursuits. If you're not quite sure about lessons or they aren't, consider an instrument and videos to teach them how to play. Guitars, drums or even classical instruments can pose a challenge and prove very rewarding for children to learn.

When older children have activities at home they enjoy and that challenge them, they will be more likely to stick around where supervision is available. While it's not likely you'll want to lord over them every second of the day, making sure they stay close most of the time can be quite comforting. Plus, there are a lot of hands-on, at-home pursuits your children can engage their friends in. This can also work to your advantage in helping you learn more about who your older kids hang out with and just what they like to do in their spare time.

If your kids would rather spend their after-school time out of the house, but organized activities don't appeal, volunteerism can provide another alternative to tap into their energy in a positive way.

VOLUNTEERING TEACHES LIFELONG SKILLS

Encouraging older children to volunteer is an incredibly smart way to help them make their free-time more productive. Depending on the activity they pursue, they can gain major life skills from the prospect. Volunteering can also help your older children out in a number of other ways.

The benefits of encouraging older children to volunteer cannot be stressed enough. When kids learn to give back, they:

- **Will gain rewards from the experience**
  Volunteering can provide some incredible rewards for those who do so. Not only will children be kept engaged in the afternoon hours, but they can also gain a tremendous amount of character out of the process. Volunteering is personally rewarding, which can build self-esteem. It is also very often quite humbling, which is never a bad experience for a preteen or teen.

- **Will meet graduation requirements**
  Many school systems are requiring X amount of community service hours before they will let children graduate. While this can take the fun out of the experience for teens, it doesn't have to. If they choose the right experience for their volunteer hours, they can have fun, gain the character rewards and get their graduation requirements taken care of all at once.

- **Will gain something for college applications**
  Volunteering can look very good on college applications.

There are lots of volunteer activities that older children can take part in. From regular daily or weekly activities to special events, there are plenty of things you can help them get involved in. Some of the more popular options for teens include:

- **Volunteering at schools**
  Older children can be valuable volunteers at elementary schools. They can read with youngsters, help them at math or simply serve as role models. Many school systems have created partnership programs that preteens and teens can sign up for in the afternoons.

- **Hospitals**
  It's a classic opportunity for older kids, but it's one that can teach them a lot about responsibility, compassion and caring. Working at a hospital as a volunteer is a rewarding way for teens to give back and learn a life lesson or two. This option is not necessarily the best for all teens, but it's one they might want to consider.

- **Nursing homes**
  While younger children might only be able to make an occasional stop at a nursing home, teens can make it a part of their routine. This volunteering option for teens can teach them more lessons that can be described. Spending time with residents can help older children learn about history, compassion, healthcare, aging and more. The rewards from this volunteer opportunity can be amazing, too.

- **Food banks or soup kitchens**
  Older children can also give back to those who are less fortunate. Volunteering at homeless shelters, soup kitchens, food banks and other similar locations will help them learn to better appreciate what they have in life.

- **Environmental actions**
  Teens are often highly encouraged to take part in environmental volunteerism. The opportunities here range from actual organized clubs to simple cleanup efforts. The value from these pursuits cannot be understated. Not only will older children learn about the issues facing the environment, they can also discover just how they can make a profound difference in their own communities.

Volunteering is an excellent way to expose older children to the world around them. It can help them see the needs that are out there, learn more about life and even teach them that they can make a difference.

ORGANIZED ACTIVITIES KEEP TEENS BUSY AND 'COOL'

Older children might like to go solo with their after-school activities or just hang out with mom and dad, but this is often not the case. Sometimes to really get them involved in an activity that's rewarding, healthy and engaging, the only option is going more structured and organized.

There are lots of options on the organized front that can keep teens active and busy a good chunk of their time. The possibilities range from one-on-one pursuits to team-based activities that can make a real difference after school.

When selecting more organized activities for older children, do make sure they are involved in the process. Trying to typecast a teen that doesn't want to be typecast can open up a whole can of worms that most parents would rather not deal with. Keep in mind that not every teen will have the same ideas when it comes to what's fun and what's rewarding. Most teens, however, can find something they enjoy doing after school that goes beyond just watching television.

Some of the options on the more organized, supervised front include:

- **Sports**
  School-based or community-based sporting activities can be fantastic for filling up after-school hours with safe, structured fun. If older children are so inclined, the options here can run year-round, too. They can take up a different sport for each season. From football and baseball to hockey and wrestling, sporting activities can really keep them going. It's even possible to engage them in sporting activities that are not team based by nature. Tennis, swimming, golfing, horseback riding and gymnastics, for example, can still give them something to do that challenges and teaches valuable life lessons. No matter the sport or sports older children pursue, these activities will teach them about disciple, goal setting and self-discipline. Even "solo" sports can help them with team work to an extent, as well.

- **Musical pursuits**
  Helping them create or take part in a band, giving them actual one-on-one lessons with a pro and other similar musical pursuits can provide an excellent way to keep older children occupied in the after-school hours. Music can give them a chance to express themselves while they learn great skills to take on to college and beyond.

- **Structured courses**
  Budding artists, photographers, dancers and so on often enjoy
  taking classes geared toward their interest. After-school pursuits in
  this vein will keep them busy, but having fun and learning at the
  same time. These can also help them develop a sense of self while
  enabling them to hone talents or interests.

- **Clubs**
  School-based clubs, Scouting, church or religious clubs and other
  similar activities can also serve older children extremely well. Clubs
  will give them a sense of belonging while helping them forge
  friendships and develop skills they can take with them into adult
  life.

Structured, organized after-school activities for older children can help
them feel a sense of belonging and accomplishment. They can also assist
preteens and teens in discovering more about who they are as people,
what they enjoy and what they are good at. As they do all these things,
these activities can give you the peace of mind you need to know your
older child is busy, having fun and learning a whole lot in the process.

UNIVERSAL ACTIVITIES FOR THE WHOLE FAMILY

After school hours don't always have to be filled with highly planned, organized sports or other similar pursuits. Sometimes it's just nice to kick back as a family and spend time together. It doesn't matter how many children live in a household or what their ages are, there are plenty of things that can be done together that will not only be enjoyable, but that can also help strengthen the bonds of family.

When family time is made a priority during the week and on the weekends, everyone will benefit. While it might not seem so right now, the years of being together are fleeting. Taking advantage of every opportunity to bond, share and enjoy each other's company will make memories that last and provide opportunities lessons that no one else besides you can teach your children. Besides, when you take time out to spend as a family, you show your kids they are, in fact, the most important people in your life.

The ideas for family activities can run a pretty wide spectrum. From just relaxing and reading together to playing sports in the backyard, you don't have to spend a lot of money to enjoy real quality time together. It's even possible to tackle home improvement projects together with everyone pitching in. If "work" is approached in the right manner, your kids will have fun even if they don't want to admit it!

Let's explore some great low-cost activities for families of any size to consider.

THE POWER OF READING

In the grand scheme of things, there might not be a family activity that can prove more valuable to your children – no matter their ages – than reading. When you make this a priority as a family starting right out of the gate, it can become a hobby you can continue to pursue together as your children grow up. While your tactics and style might need to change based on your children's ages, this hobby can be a family affair for certain. Plus, it can provide some incredible memories that will last a lifetime.

Some strategies to consider using for developing reading as family hobby include:

- **Reading out loud**
  While you will have to start in this manner with younger children no matter what, the practice can continue as your kids age. When they become readers, you can ask them to read to you to practice their oral skills. You can even switch off reading passages in books to each other. Select a great story the whole family can enjoy and you and older children can work together to read it aloud to younger children. Reading special books or short stories aloud can also be worked into holiday traditions. Reciting a special holiday short story, for example, can become a cherished memory for children as they grow up.

- **Reading together**
  When your children get older, you can read together without reading out loud. This is still quality family time and it will show your kids that you place a high value on this pursuit.

- **Creating your own "book club"**
  Get multiple copies of the books your children are reading in school or just for pleasure and create your own book club. Once the family is finished reading a particular title, you can all get together and discuss the book, its characters, themes and even questions your children might have. This is an excellent way to spend after-school time and it can prove very valuable for helping your children develop critical thinking skills.

Inspire a love of reading in your children early and help them carry it through life and the rewards will be amazing. While it might seem like reading is a solitary pursuit, it doesn't have to be. You can make it a family affair if you use the right tactics.

<u>BACKYARD SPORTS</u>

Reading is fantastic and its benefits cannot be stressed enough, but sometimes you just want to get physical. Your family can take advantage of after-school time to encourage sportsmanship, exercise or both without necessarily having to enroll kids in organized activities. There are, in fact, a number of things you can do in your own backyard and neighborhood that will encourage children of all ages to get involved, get active and have some fun in the process.

Some of the things you can do together that will develop a sense of family fun while getting everyone off the couch and moving include:

- **Baseball**
  If your neighborhood has the room or your backyard does, a little game of ball can be a whole lot of fun to work into regular routine. Make provisions for younger players. If a full game isn't possible, consider just working on catching and throwing, batting and bunting.

- **Basketball**
  Throwing hoops can be enjoyed by family members of just about any age. If children are older, one-on-one or two-on-two games can be a real blast that will get the blood pumping and the family spirit going.

- **Croquette**
  This is an oldie, but a goodie. This particular game is such that kids of any age can get involved. You won't break a huge sweat playing, but it does beat couch time.

- **Bike rides, walks or runs**
  Exploring the neighborhood on foot or by bike is a great way to enjoy some time together off the couch and out of the house. This can help kids get more active while providing a great opportunity for the family to bond.

- **Swimming**
  If you do have access to a backyard pool or a community pools, this can be an incredibly fun activity for the entire family. Swimming is not only an excellent way to exercise, it can also be an important skill to pass on to young children. Having the ability to swim can save lives.

Just about any sport or physical pursuit can be altered to become a family game or event. The important thing is finding something everyone enjoys and is willing to take part in. Activities can be competitive in nature or just performed for the pure joy involved. Do what works best for you and your kids and your entire family will benefit from going outside and getting active.

HOME IMPROVEMENT 101

Family time doesn't have to be all about sports, games and reading. You can actually put kids to work and still have a great time in the process. If you play your cards right, you can get your children to help out around the house or even in the neighborhood and they might not even realize they are "working."

So, how can you get some actual work done and get your kids to willingly help out? Depending on their ages, there are a number of tactics you can employ. Some ideas for getting them going without having to bribe them include:

- **Making cleaning day game day**
  When it's time to clean up the house from top to bottom, turning it into a fun adventure can be an excellent way to get the kids to pitch in. Turn on the radio and tune it in to your kids' favorite station. Sing, dance and clean as you go. Assign them jobs, create "cleaning teams" and even give out prizes to the team that finishes their tasks first.

- **Dinnertime chores**
  If eating dinner together every night or at least a few nights a week is a priority, turn these occasions into full family events. Get the kids involved in planning the meals, preparing them and setting the table. Even consider letting them pick out a dessert and pitching in to make it. Do keep in-kitchen tasks age-appropriate, but you'd be amazed at how much little ones can actually help out. Older children are often thrilled to learn how to be more self-sufficient in the kitchen, too.

- **Crafting home improvement projects with care**
  If there is a need to do a big job around the house, you can get the kids involved in many cases. Say you want to build a barbecue pit in the backyard, turn the project into an entire family affair. Younger kids can help with clearing the yard while older children might be able to get involved with the actual design and construction. Consider sitting down with the entire family to brainstorm projects of this nature. The kids are more likely to get more involved if they helped pick the project and worked on its planning.

- **Gardening**
  This is an excellent home improvement project that won't really

seem like work if you play your cards right. Children of all ages can enjoy and benefit from learning how to grow their own vegetables, flowers or other ornamental plants. Plus, if you choose to go with edible gardening, your family will reap the rewards of its labors in a tasty way, too! Gardening can teach your children responsibility, help them hone their math skills and even assist in the science classroom, as well.

- **Teach them to assist older neighbors**
  Getting kids to help other people is often a little easier than getting them to work at home. If your family has put a priority on helping elderly neighbors, for example, do engage your children in the pursuit. It's more "fun" for kids to dust shelves for a kind neighbor lady than to do it at home.

Getting children more actively involved in the family can take a little time and effort on your part, but it can pay off for you and your kids in the long run. When you come up with things to do together after school or just on the weekends, your family time will become more special and you can create memories that will last a lifetime without costing a fortune in the process. Even very simple activities like reading and cleaning the house can be turned into enjoyable moments spent together.

PARTING WORDS OF ADVICE

Studies have shown that children who are engaged in constructive activities after-school tend to stay out of trouble and even learn skills they can take with them throughout life. Finding the right activities for you and your children can require some patience and experimentation, but the work can pay off for everyone involved.

Whether you intend to enroll your kids in organized, after-school activities or you just want to keep them busy at home, do keep their unique interests in mind. When you help them cultivate the interests they already have and expose them to new opportunities, your children will grow.

After-school activities do not have to cost a small fortune to have lasting, important impacts on youngsters. Reading, joining clubs and even learning to help out through volunteerism can all offer important lessons for children no matter their age.

While it's often best to get kids engaged in activities at least at home as early as possible, it's never too late to help them develop their personal interests. The time spent once homework is done and chores are completed can be filled with so much more if you assist your children in exploring their options and following their interests. Chance are strong that if you help them select something that really appeals to them, your child and your family will benefit as a result.

Thank you for purchasing this book. Your business is much appreciated.

For more planners, journals, diaries and books I offer,

find me at https://amzn.to/2EjtX8C

or for digital printables, ebooks and other fun items

join me at https://dianekurzava.etsy.com

Connect with me at:

https://dknaturalluxury.com

Learn more at:

Http://natural-luxury.teachable.com

Start your own laptop lifestyle business:

Free Webinar HERE!